A MIGRANT FAMILY

A MIGRANT FAMILY

Text and Photographs by Larry Dane Brimner

Lerner Publications Company / Minneapolis

Interviews and photography for this book were completed during the spring and summer of 1991. Additional photographs are reproduced courtesy of: pp. 1, 11 (right), 40, *San Diego Union/* Michael Franklin; p. 10, *San Diego Union/* Charlie Neuman.

Library of Congress Cataloging-in-Publication Data

Brimner, Larry Dane.
    A migrant family / text and photographs by Larry Dane Brimner.
        p.   cm.
    Includes bibliographical references.
    Summary: Portrays the life of twelve-year-old Juan Medina and his family, migrant workers living in Encinitas, California.
    ISBN 0-8225-2554-2
    1. Migrant agricultural laborers—California—Encinitas—Juvenile literature. 2. Children of migrant laborers—California—Encinitas—Juvenile literature. 3. Family—California—Encinitas—Juvenile literature. [1. Migrant labor. 2. Agricultural laborers. 3. Mexican Americans. 4. Medina, Juan.] I. Title.
HD1527.C2B75   1992
305.5'63—dc20   91-27019
                                                                CIP
                                                                AC

Manufactured in the United States of America

2 3 4 5 6 7 8 9 10 – P/JR – 02 00 99 98 97 96 95 94

Author's Note

Many people helped with the writing of this book. I wish to thank Gloria Carranza and Raymond Muñoz for introducing me to Juan; the San Dieguito Union High School District, especially Margie Bulkin and Mercedes Capurso, for allowing me into Juan's school and answering my questions; Central Union High School's Barbara Oswalt and Gerardo Roman for opening their doors so that I might take photos; and the many migrant people who warmly welcomed me into *el monte* to share their stories with me.

A special thanks to Joel and Teresa Ruiz for their graciousness and openness.

But it is to Juan Medina that I owe the most gratitude. Muchas gracias, Juan, y deseos para una gran vida.

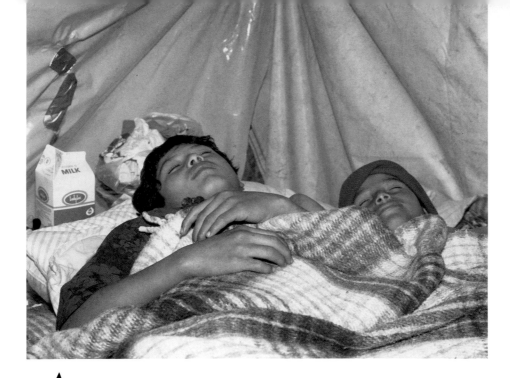

As darkness bleeds from the sky, Juan shivers at the 6:00 A.M. chill. The 12-year-old tugs at the blanket, wishing for a little more warmth and a few extra minutes of sleep. But it's no use. The blanket he shares with his brothers, eight-year-old Alejandro and four-year-old Martin, is just as quickly snatched back, so Juan stretches and gives in to another day.

Juan Medina is used to getting up with the sun. "Es el reloj de alarma," he explains in Spanish. Then in English he interprets: "Alarm clock." He nods toward a sliver of sun peeking above the California hillside and buries his bare hands in his pockets.

Juan Medina rises early
each morning.

Juan is a migrant. He was born in Mexico, but he has lived in Indiana, Illinois, and Iowa, where his stepfather, Joel Ruiz, has worked on farms. For the last three years, however, Juan and his family have been in California. During the winter and spring, they stay in the coastal community of Encinitas, near San Diego. Juan's stepfather works as a day laborer—someone hired for one day's work at a time—in construction, harvesting flowers, or doing odd jobs. But when it's time to pick melons, tomatoes, and other crops, the family heads north to Fresno, a city in California's great Central Valley.

Just as migratory birds fly north or south depending on the season and the weather, migrant farm workers have their own patterns of migration. For these people, it is the promise of earning minimum wages that keeps them on the move. Workers and their families trek to *el norte* (the north) as the days grow warmer and the crops reach their peak. There is food to be pulled from the ground or plucked from the trees and vines, and migrant farm workers provide the muscle to do the pulling and plucking. When a job is done, they move on to the next crop and the next harvest in an annual cycle.

The family's "kitchen counter"

Using whatever scraps of material they can scavenge, the migrant workers build shelters among the trees and undergrowth.

Juan and his family live in a camp along El Camino Real, a major highway that links Southern California's coastal communities. The hillside above the road is dotted with expensive houses that have red-tiled roofs and electric security gates. But Juan's house, like those of the 300 other people in the camp, doesn't have a red-tiled roof. Here, houses are built of salvaged plywood. Orange or blue sheets of plastic make do for roofs. Trees and chaparral (shrubs and underbrush) shelter the crude shacks.

A migrant camp is set up in the brush. Opposite: Anything can serve as shelter—blinds make do for a wall, and some workers sleep in a "spider hole" in the ground.

The migrant workers call the camps in the scrubby growth *"el monte,"* or "the brush." There are more than 200 such camps in the San Diego area. Their populations range in size from just a few people to many hundred. Only about 40 of the camps are registered with the state of California and meet minimum health and safety regulations. The other camps spring up wherever workers find empty land, and these sites usually lack drinking water, electricity, and toilets.

Juan and his brothers sleep on an old mattress—which they found at a swap meet—atop a plywood platform. Juan's mother, stepfather, and two-year-old sister Carmela sleep on a similar platform on the opposite side of the shelter. The floor is dirt.

Just outside the shack, a piece of lumber leaning against the wall supports several carefully tended orchids. Tonight's dinner, beans, already simmers over an open fire. A new mountain bike is propped against a tree trunk. The bicycle, a Christmas gift from an anonymous donor, is for everyone in *el monte* to use. But these days, the kids don't get to ride very often; rains have turned the dense thicket where they live into a muddy slough. Teresa, Juan's mother, also worries that the cars that speed along El Camino Real make the road too dangerous for bicycles. Already, several people have been struck as they tried to cross the roadway.

Juan threads his way through the brush and dashes across El Camino Real to the other side, where portable toilets are set up for migrant workers and their families. As he washes the sleep from his eyes at a cold-water faucet, Juan hears the food truck trumpet its horn. At once men, women, and children begin to flow out of the camp and across the road. Juan wipes his face against his shoulder, dries his hands on his pants, and checks his pockets. He withdraws a crumpled dollar bill and some change. Hurrying to the truck, he asks for orange juice and a honey bun as his neighbors crowd around to get their own breakfasts.

Back in the camp, Juan and his family stand around the fire and eat what they've purchased from the catering truck. From time to time, neighbors pass by and exchange news. It's rumored that a nearby farmer will be looking for extra workers to pick strawberries. Somebody else mentions that a construction company will be hiring as many as 20 workers to help with a housing project. A fence company might need someone to dig holes.

The community is close-knit. Juan and his family know every face in the camp. News of possible work is shared freely and people look out for each other. But late last night, there was trouble. Two young white men, or *Anglos*, entered the camp and roughed up one of the migrant workers. One of the men held a knife to the worker's neck while the other ransacked his shelter. They stole the $300 the worker had saved to send back to his wife and children in Mexico. Then, before leaving, one of the Anglos made a slur that was as sharp as his knife: "Wetback."

Juan flinches at the word *wetback*, an insult used to describe workers who sneak across the border from Mexico to find work. "We have papers," he says. "We have a right to be here. Who are we hurting?"

He doesn't expect anyone to answer. He has gotten used to the insults and threats. They go along with being a migrant worker. But he is quick to point out that almost everyone in the camp is in the United States legally.

Even so, the theft of $300 will not be reported to the sheriff. Most migrant workers do not trust American law enforcement agencies. The workers fear that if they report a crime or get into trouble--even if they are the victims—they might land in jail or be forced out of the United States. The migrants will handle this incident themselves: from now on, they will post lookouts to stand watch.

There is another rumor going around. People in the expensive houses in the hills have complained about the lack of sanitation in the camp and the danger of fire if the trees and chaparral turn dry. County authorities may order the camp destroyed. Juan worries that this might be more than a rumor; he knows it has happened before. Many camps were cited by the county health department for health-code violations this year. Bulldozers flattened the camps, leaving the migrant workers only with what they were wearing or what they could salvage.

"They want us to work," Juan says. "And they want us to disappear."

No one knows for certain how many migrants there are across the United States. Statistics are hard to come by because migrant workers and their children move so often. Some estimates say there are as many as five million migrants in the U.S., and perhaps a half-million school-age migrant children. The majority of migrant workers are Hispanic or black. Often they speak little or no English and lack other job skills.

According to the Regional Task Force on the Homeless, more than 50,000 migrant workers and their families live legally in San Diego County in California. Because of the county's location near Mexico, most of the migrants in the county are Hispanic, like Juan.

Field labor is back-breaking work.

The Immigration Reform and Control Act of 1986 made it legal for seasonal workers to remain in the United States if they could prove that they had worked and lived there regularly. It also gave the workers the chance to qualify for full U.S. citizenship. During peak harvest seasons, however, thousands of others cross the U.S. border illegally from Mexico to take up life in the camps of *el monte* and to seek work.

The traditional migrant worker is a male who travels by himself to where the work is and sends the money he earns to his family. But according to Gloria Carranza, Transients Issues Coordinator for the city of Encinitas, more and more families are joining their working fathers and sons. Even though it's hard to live on a minimum-wage salary, it's still more money than a family could earn in many Mexican and Central American villages. In their home countries, many migrants faced extreme poverty. It was difficult, if not impossible, to find work, and people lived without electricity or running water.

Ten years ago, most Southern California residents barely knew that workers and their camps existed. Then came the exploding population and the building boom of the early 1980s. New housing developments bordered worker camps. Workers began to cut through residential lots on their way to the fields. Passing motorists came face to face with workers lined up along suburban streets waiting for job offers. Migrants were no longer invisible.

In communities with large migrant populations, tensions run high. People who have paid a half-million dollars for a house with a view don't like to look out over a sea of plastic and cardboard shacks. The wealthy residents often complain. They see migrants as dirty and lazy and say they don't fit in with the larger community. Migrants, on the other hand, say they're rarely asked to join the larger community and that they do the kinds of jobs that nobody else will do.

Young migrant workers wait along the street for offers of work.

Most migrants are honest, hardworking people. Yet they are commonly blamed for almost all the crimes that occur in an area near where the migrants live or gather. And it's not unusual to hear people describe migrant workers as illegal aliens—foreigners living in the U.S. illegally—even though the Immigration and Naturalization Service (INS) estimates that 50 to 80 percent of workers in the camps live in the United States legally.

Some people try to explain the conditions in the camps by saying that migrants don't want to live any other way. Juan's stepfather, Joel, scoffs at that notion. "Who would want to live like this, my friend?" he asks. "Your pets have better."

Migrants don't live in the camps by choice. They simply don't make enough money to find decent housing. Sometimes they don't get paid at all. According to Claudia Smith, a lawyer with California Rural Legal Assistance (CRLA), a migrants' rights group, about three-fourths of the 800 cases her office handled in the previous year involved wages not being paid to migrants. Workers have no choice but to live in the camps when they aren't paid the money they are due, she says.

Perhaps what bothers many Americans is that migrants are a reminder of a national embarrassment. It's difficult to understand how, in a country with so much wealth, some people have so little.

Joel didn't set out to live in *el monte*, but employers seldom provide housing for workers, and rents are expensive. With security deposits, it can cost $2,000 or more just to move into a small apartment. Monthly rent might be $800 or more. It is hard to save that kind of money. But Joel says that life in *el monte* is still better than what he had in Mexico. He can earn in one day in the U.S. what would have taken him months to earn in Mexico. And there is something more. "Here," he says, "I have hope—if not for me, then for my children."

Teresa,
Joel, Alejandro,
and Carmela

He tries to put aside a little money each week. Some weeks this is impossible, though, because he may not find work every day. And when he does find a job, he can't always count on getting paid. "The check"—Joel pretends to dribble an imaginary basketball as he explains—"many times it bounces." He means that the paychecks turn out to be worthless.

For migrant workers who are in the United States illegally, there is something else to worry about. Some employers hire illegal workers on purpose, promising to pay them in cash at the end of the day. Instead, the employer calls the INS as soon as the job is finished. Border Patrol and INS agents meet the workers at the job site and shuttle them back to their native country. The employer gets the job done for nothing.

Workers stoop over to plant a field.

In an effort to soothe homeowners and merchants who complain about the large number of migrants along the streets, the city of Encinitas has opened the Encinitas Jobs Center. The Jobs Center operates out of a mobile van and provides employers with legal workers who are eager for temporary or permanent employment.

Raymond Muñoz, who staffs the Jobs Center, calls it a win-win situation. "The number of migrants along the streets has been reduced," he says. "At the same time, both employers and workers are afforded a certain amount of protection. Employers can be sure that our workers are legitimately looking for a job and not trouble, while workers are less likely to be taken advantage of when they receive a job through the center."

In addition to its employment services, the Jobs Center puts workers in touch with other community agencies. A program is underway to encourage migrants to open savings accounts in local banks. Library cards have been issued, and many workers now make regular trips to the library. The center also offers help with income tax preparation.

Muñoz encourages workers who are waiting for jobs to participate in the English classes offered outdoors at the center each morning. "Many of them know that the best way to move into more steady employment is to improve their English," he explains.

Joel is very enthusiastic about the program. "English is *muy necesario*, very necessary," he says, tousling Juan's hair.

"I study," Juan protests, ducking away from Joel's playful hand.

Like most young people, Juan dreams about being rich. "Someday," he says, "I will live in a house like that." His gaze is fixed on one of the large houses perched above the Jobs Center. "But first, school."

Juan sits on a tree stump as he waits for the school bus. From time to time, he checks his jeans pocket to make sure the dollar his step-father gave him for lunch is still there. A blond girl joins him at the unmarked bus stop. She doesn't speak to him. Juan looks the other way.

A few moments later, when the bus rumbles up, the girl bounds up the steps and into the noisy crowd. Juan lags behind. "Her mother spit on me the first time I caught the bus here," he says, looking toward the girl. "Her mother did not want me around her." He shrugs. "I did not pick the bus stop."

At Digueño Junior High School, Juan usually keeps to himself. The few friends he has are other migrant children. He likes soccer, though. "You don't have to speak English to play the soccer," he admits.

English is not easy for Juan because he has never lived in one place long enough to learn it well, and in the places he's lived, almost everyone spoke Spanish. Some of Juan's classes, such as history and science, are taught in Spanish. But he also has a two-hour daily block of English.

Migrant children often enter school unprepared, and moving around so often makes them fall behind. They might be asked to help out with younger brothers and sisters on the days when both parents find work. Also, many migrant children begin working as soon as they are old enough to contribute to the family income. The result is that they get further and further behind in school. Juan has been luckier than most: his mother and stepfather tell him that his studies come first.

The dropout rate is high for migrant children. In some parts of California, as many as 70 percent of migrant children do not finish high school, and statewide the average is about 20 percent. The national average is 50 percent. What this means is that across the United States, 5 out of every 10 migrant children eventually drop out of school.

Migrant children face unique problems in school. Teachers often give up on them because they attend a particular school for only a brief time. Other students may view migrants as outsiders and not take the time to make friends with them. Some migrant children get lost in the system—they move so frequently that schools lose their records.

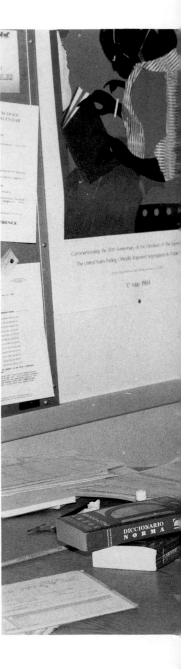

These migrant students receive special tutoring at school.

Mercedes Capurso works with Digueño Junior High's migrant students and their families. When a migrant is absent, Capurso visits his or her home to find out why. She arranges for medical attention if it's needed and helps parents understand the importance of education.

"Many migrant parents do not read or write even their native language," Capurso observes. "It takes personal contact with them to explain how the schools can help their children." She sees to it that Digueño's migrant students are headed in the right direction by signing them up for the classes they should take.

Margie Bulkin, Digueño's bilingual resource teacher, says many of the migrant children have not had a chance to do simple things like visit a zoo or eat in a restaurant or go to a dance. Bulkin organizes field trips and other activities for them. This year Juan went on a school trip to San Diego's Wild Animal Park to see African animals in a natural setting.

To show migrant students that they have options, Capurso and Bulkin match them with lunchtime tutors from nearby colleges. The tutors, former migrants themselves who are now attending college, offer academic help and more –they are proof that education is the way out of *el monte*.

Attitudes are difficult to change. The attitudes that divide the community of Encinitas are present at school also. "Schools reflect the feelings of the community," Bulkin comments. It's not uncommon, for example, to find migrant students clustered in one circle and Anglos in another. To foster an understanding between the two groups, the school has organized a series of roundtable discussions.

"It's better now," Juan says. "When people talk, they get to know each other. Ignorance is a bad thing. It makes people not like each other."

All day, Juan has worried about the rumor that the camp where his family is staying might be demolished. As his bus grinds to a stop, he looks nervously out the window. Huge bulldozers stand idle in the field. A trash bin overflows with splintered wood, torn tarpaulins, and an assortment of household goods. The rumor was true.

Juan pushes out of the bus and races across the field. Joel, Teresa, Carmela, Alejandro, and Martin sit on an old railroad tie waiting for him. No one sheds tears. To be a migrant is to move.

The family spends the next few days collecting building materials. They go to the swap meet to buy used items. In the early-morning hours, they walk the streets looking through people's trash before the city sanitation crew hauls away anything useful. Juan is concerned about missing so much school, but he must help rebuild.

By the end of the week, the workers have built a new camp in another part of *el monte*. This camp is nearer to the market, but it's a two-mile hike to the drinking water and toilets near the Jobs Center. Teresa looks at the new surroundings. "It is much drier," she says, giving Carmela a bottle of milk. Now she and the children won't have to slosh through mud.

The old camp was destroyed, but
a new one is set up.

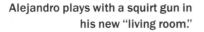
Alejandro plays with a squirt gun in his new "living room."

It is a crisp morning, and Joel is up early to check in at the Jobs Center. Martin and Alejandro take turns sitting and spinning in an easy chair. They play with a squirt gun. Both the chair and the plastic squirt gun are scavenged treasures. Joel flashes a smile and shows his sense of humor. "How do you like our new apartment?" he asks. "*Muy elegante—* very elegant—no?" Then he sets off into the brush. The Jobs Center is no longer just across the street. "Juan!" he shouts.

Juan scurries out of the lean-to with his school notebook. "I have missed too much," he says. "Too much." As he hurries to catch up with Joel, a sliver of sun peeks above the California hillside. Darkness slowly bleeds from the sky.

For Further Reading

Ashabranner, Brent. *Dark Harvest: Migrant Farmworkers in America.* New York: Dodd, Mead & Co., 1985.

Emmet, Herman LeRoy. *Fruit Tramps: A Family of Migrant Farmworkers.* Albuquerque: University of New Mexico Press, 1989.

Roberts, Naurice. *Cesar Chavez and La Causa.* Chicago: Children's Press, 1986.